W9-CTN-632

Catholic

IS

Wonderful!

How to Make the Most of It

Mitch Finley

Resurrection Press
Mineola • New York

Other books by Mitch Finley:

Christian Families in the Real World (with Kathy Finley; Thomas More Press).

Catholic Spiritual Classics (Sheed & Ward)

Time Capsules of the Church (Our Sunday Visitor Books)

Your Family in Focus: Appreciating What You Have, Making It Even Better (Ave Maria Press)

Everybody Has a Guardian Angel...And Other Lasting Lessons I Learned in Catholic Schools (Crossroad Publishing Co.)

Heavenly Helpers: St. Anthony and St. Jude (Crossroad Publishing Co.)

All quotations from scripture are from the New Revised Standard Version Bible: Catholic Edition, Copyright 1989, 1993, Division of Christian Education of the National Council of the Churches of Christ in the United States of America.

First published in 1994 by Resurrection Press, Ltd.
P.O. Box 248
Williston Park, NY 11596

ISBN: 1-878718-24-X

Cover design: Roth Advertising, Inc.

Printed in the United States of America.

Dedication

THIS BOOK is for our three sons, Sean Thomas, Patrick Daniel, and Kevin Andrew, to whom I say: Guys, as your father I reserve the right to give you advice. It's in the fatherly job description. You may ask, "Why should we stay Catholic as we grow up?" Just this, I would reply: We live in a mixed-up world, a world where there is much good, plenty of bad, and a lot of confusing stuff in-between. If you would keep your bearings you need a compass. Your Catholic faith is that compass. Your Catholic faith will give you trustworthy values and ideals, it will keep you in touch with God's love and help you discover the truth of your own deepest self.

Regardless of what you do or where you go, your Catholic faith will help you be a person others will be happy to know. Your faith won't save you from suffering, but it will help you to not whine about it so much. Your faith will bring more joy into your life than you would otherwise have, and when you feel that joy, you'll know Who to thank. There are countless phony gods that look very attractive, but they can never be trusted; if you believe their lies they will lead you into more grief and misery than you can imagine.

Live your Catholic faith, be a prayerful person, and you will have a life worth living. That's advice you can take to the bank. I promise.

Love, Dad

Contents

Foreword

CATHOLICISM is a messy and confusing religion in part because it strives to embrace everyone and in part because in its willingness to embrace everyone it is willing to embrace every possible custom. Moreover it changes its customs periodically and without warning.

It would be so nice, one often thinks, if there were only one kind of Catholicism everywhere in the world. If we are going to have celibacy, for example, we must not permit Byzantine priests to marry. If we are going to hold hands while reciting the Lord's Prayer at the Eucharist, let us mandate this custom in every church in the Catholic world. If we want frequent confessions again, let us outlaw the Easter and Christmas penitential services. If we are going to permit annulments, let us make the rules and procedures the same everywhere in the world. If we really worry about unity, let us go back to having the Mass in one language, any one language no matter what it is. Let us have guitar Masses everywhere or no where. Let us abolish all the fringe elements like the Catholic charismatics. Let us denounce all Catholic groups that presume to criticize Church authorities. Let us go back to a time when it was clear to everyone just what a Catholic had to believe and had to do.

Above all let us get rid of those who don't fit. Let us purge all those who practice birth control or who think women ought to be priests. Or, alternatively, let us follow the advice of those who want us to be a "counter-culture" and concentrate on being different from other materialist, secularist, consumerist Americans. Let us rather concentrate all our energies (such as we have left after getting rid of the undesirables) on serving the poor and the oppressed, especially those who are politically correct.

None of this is about to happen, of course. Catholicism is by its very nature pluralistic. As a great Catholic novelist (who wasn't sure how Catholic he was) wrote once, Here Comes Everybody. Let all the customs blossom, let all styles be welcome, let's stretch the boundaries out as far as we can and see whom we come up with.

There are outer limits. But the Catholic religious enterprise, at least in its better moments, has not defined those limits too rigidly or too exclusively.

Peter Rossi, my mentor, once remarked that he left the Church when he was twelve and woke up one morning when he was forty to discover that he was Catholic again. This wasn't because he had changed but because the Church, without giving (him) any advanced warning, had extended its boundaries out so far that now he was included.

I told him that he had always been included, but he wouldn't believe me. He still, by the way, usually eats fish on Friday.

We are now at a time in Catholic history when the counter-Reformation is coming to an end, when the pluralism (and resultant messiness) is increasing rather than decreasing. If Catholicism was never as simple as it used to seem, it now appears more variegated than it has ever been.

In this confused situation, Mitch Finley tries to tease out some of the major components of the Catholic tradition. It is not an easy task, because one cannot reduce Catholicism to a single norm (be it papal infallibility or liberation theology). Yet Mr. Finley has the right "feel" for the Catholic heritage. In this book he does the very good work of sharing that feel with the rest of us, not perhaps so much to teach us anything new about our tradition, but rather confirm what we already know or at least strongly suspect.

Andrew M. Greeley
Grand Beach, Michigan
June 5, 1994

Why Stay Catholic?

THOMAS MERTON, who died in 1968, is probably the 20th century's most influential American Catholic writer. In his 1966 book, *Conjectures of a Guilty Bystander,* the famous Trappist monk quoted the French novelist and philosopher Albert Camus. "An oriental wise man," Camus wrote, "always used to ask the Divinity in his prayers to be so kind as to spare him from living in an interesting era. As we are not wise, the Divinity has not spared us, and we are living in an interesting era."

You can say that again, Al. One of the more interesting characteristics of our era is that many Catholics today wonder if they should remain Catholic. Some Catholics get frustrated with this or that about the church, and the next thing you know they join some other church or religious group, or they opt for religious indifference. Most Catholics remain Catholic, of course, but some join everything from the Rev. Sun Myung Moon's "Moonies" to a local New Age church; everything from fundamentalist Bible churches to the Mormons.

Time was, Catholics gave no thought to staying Catholic. Most Catholics who were born Catholic stayed Catholic. Sure, many families had the family "lapsed Catholic." But even a lapsed Catholic still thought of himself or herself as a Catholic, and so did everyone else. Someone asked the great Irish writer, James Joyce, a "fallen-away" Catholic, if he had become a Protestant. "Good God!" Joyce replied. "I've lost my faith, not my mind!"

Today, it's not unusual for many Catholics to ponder the question, Why stay Catholic? A rhetorical question bandied about a good deal asks, "Isn't one church as good as the next?"

To which I would reply: No and yes. As a Catholic who loves being Catholic, I'm biased. I think being Catholic is wonderful. Like many Catholics, I disagree with a few official, non-essential, church teachings. Like most Catholics, I do not believe that every papal or Vatican pronouncement is virtually, if not literally, infallible. But Catholicism is in my blood, it's almost genetic. I wouldn't be anything else.

That's my subjective response. My objective response is historical, and the historical facts are clear. The Roman Catholic Church has direct historical ties to the apostles of Jesus and the first Christian communities. (The Eastern Orthodox churches can make a similar claim, but I don't have the space to discuss that here.) At one time or another, all other churches broke away from Catholicism, from a group that broke away from Catholicism, or from a group that broke away from a group that broke away, and so on.

In addition, the Roman Catholic Church is linked historically to the first Christian communities whose faith experience and Sacred Tradition gave birth to the New Testament. To be in communion with the Roman Catholic Church is to be as close as you can get to the spiritual source of the New Testament itself.

This does not mean that Martin Luther, or any of the other 16th-century Protestant reformers, didn't have some legitimate gripes. They certainly did, and it's a shame the Catholic Church of that era couldn't hear what Luther, Calvin, Zwingli, and the others said and avoid the tragic divisions that took place. At the same time, the Protestant Reformers made some mistakes, too, and it's a shame they couldn't be more patient instead of stomping off to start their own churches.

Because I cherish the Catholic faith, and because historically it is clear that the Roman Catholic Church is the original Christian Church, I would say that one church is not as good as the next. Still, a lot of water has gone under the bridge in the more than 500 years since the Protestant Reformation. Many generations of Christians have lived and died as Lutherans, Presbyterians, Anglicans, Baptists, and as members of groups like the Assemblies of God and the Nazarene Church. Roman Catholics believe the gift of salvation—spiritual healing and liberation—is *most fully* present in the Catholic Church. Still, salvation can come to people through whatever religious tradition they find themselves a part of or, indeed, outside of any religion. For someone whose family has been Episcopalian for generations, to remain Episcopalian may be the best thing for him or her. Someone who is Baptist may be better off staying Baptist. In this sense, it's just as good for someone else to be a Lutheran as it is for me to be a Catholic. In this subjective sense, "one church is as good as another."

If you are a Catholic, I find it difficult to imagine circumstances that would make it a good idea for you to become something else. The only exception I can think of would be if you are Catholic and your spouse belongs to another tradition. If the future health and unity of your marriage and family would be endangered if you insist on remaining a Catholic, then you may want to think about joining your spouse in his or her faith tradition. Ideally, this is an issue you work out prior to your marriage. Ecumenical or two-tradition families can be healthy, strong, and a blessing to the world, but I believe that the ideal is for husband and wife to share the same faith tradition and community.

People think of leaving the Catholic Church for various reasons. They don't like something about the church. They disagree with certain church teachings. They find their parish to be cold and impersonal, too conservative, or too liberal. They were offended or treated unkindly by a priest. They are divorced and think, mistakenly, that they can't remain Catholic and remarry. All of these reasons to "leave the church" are understandable, but they all carry the implication that the church should measure up to my standards before I will accept it. Ultimately, they all imply that the Catholic Church must be nearly perfect, *as I understand perfection*, before I will remain a Catholic.

Father Andrew M. Greeley, probably the most widely recognized American Catholic writer of the late 20th century, gave the perfect response to this point of view. If you can find a perfect church, Greeley said, go ahead and join it. But as soon as you do, it won't be perfect anymore.

Why stay Catholic? Because you're not likely to do better anyplace else. "Catholic" means "universal" or "all-encompassing." Anything good, true, and beautiful that you find outside the Catholic Church is present in the church as well, even if you must look for it for a while. Either that, or it's compatible with Catholicism and you should incorporate it yourself. You will find in Catholicism the greatest potential to experience God's self-gift, or grace. You will find in the Catholic Church the most reliable opportunity to discover the truth about yourself, about other people, about life, and about the world we live in. That's it in a nutshell.

When push comes to shove, of course, each person makes his or her own free choice to be, or not be, a Catholic. This book is for those who, like myself, decide to stay and want to make the most of a living Catholic faith, tradition, and identity.

Sometimes we can be so eager to praise what's good in other traditions that we can overlook what's special and unique about our own. This book is about appreciating and cultivating what's special about belonging to the oldest institution in the western world, the Roman Catholic Church. It's about treasuring Catholicism in ways that will benefit us, and our children and grandchildren, the most.

Chapter 1

What Kind of Catholic Are You?

IN NORTH AMERICA, more people identify themselves as Catholic than claim membership in any other single religious tradition. More than fifty-nine million citizens of the United States alone claim membership in the Roman Catholic Church. But numbers can be deceiving.

As a writer for Catholic magazines and newspapers, when I interview someone I try to discover what kind of Catholic he or she is. Practicing? Non-practicing? Liberal, conservative, moderate? Well informed about what's happening in the church today, or out of touch? Is this person a "Sunday Catholic," or does he or she try to practice the faith seven days a week?

There have always been different kinds of Catholics, socially, culturally, in terms of educational level, and in terms of their theological inclinations. But today the theological differences, in particular, are more different, if you will. Clear contrasts characterize the various groups in the church that claim to be authentically Catholic. Consequently, when someone tells me that he or she is a Catholic, I'm inclined to ask, "What do you mean by that?" The lines between the various ways of being a Catholic are difficult to draw straight, and they blur easily. For illustration purposes, however, I will hazard descriptions of the various kinds of Catholics one can find in the church today.

Some people define Catholic as being rooted in and guided by the living Catholic tradition. They are active in a parish and participate in the Eucharist, or Mass, regularly. They place a high value on the Sacraments and the Scriptures, and they make regular time for a form of prayer that suits them best including, perhaps, a traditional prayer form such as the rosary. They may subscribe to two or three national-level Catholic periodicals. They respect the pope and Vatican officials, but they don't pay much attention to what they say. Still, they are grateful for the leadership of the pope and their local bishop. These people generally agree that abortion is unacceptable. Consistent with bottom-line church teachings, they do not attribute infallibility to every official church pronouncement, and they believe they should follow the dictates of an informed adult conscience. They do not believe they are free before God to shut off their intellect and critical faculties and simply obey all official church teachings. I call such people "progressive Catholics."

Another kind of Catholic picks and chooses from the tradition even more than progressive Catholics do. Such Catholics listen when the pope says what they already agree with, but they ignore him when they disagree. They attend Mass more Sundays than not, but they have no qualms about missing Mass if it doesn't fit into their plans. They may be "pro-choice" on the abortion issue. They may have a serious commitment to social and economic justice, including church issues such as the ordination of women and married men. Such Catholics tend to sympathize with feminist concerns and be open to addressing God as both Father and Mother, and they favor the complete elimination of masculine metaphors from the Bible and liturgical texts. They may have rather free notions about sexual morality. I call such people "liberal Catholics."

Other Catholics—a significant percentage of the total Catholic population, I suspect—attend Mass most Sundays but their faith has little impact on their everyday lives, including work and family relationships. They may attend an occasional parish social or educational event, but for the most part their Catholicism is reserved for Mass on Saturday or Sunday. They may receive a diocesan newspaper if they don't have to pay for it, but they rarely read it. The liturgical seasons have little meaning for these folks beyond two days, Christmas and Easter. They are not well informed about what's happening in the church, and they make few efforts to become better informed about their faith. These people might be described as "Sunday Catholics."

Still other Catholics insist that a Catholic must agree with and follow all official papal and Vatican pronouncements. These people often believe they are the only true Catholics, that all other Catholics are wishy-washy or "cafeteria" Catholics who select according to personal whim what they want from the church instead of embracing the official Vatican perspective on Catholicism. For these people, when the Vatican speaks it might as well be God speaking. Such Catholics are "pro-life" on the abortion issue, but they may think capital punishment is a great idea. They pay close attention to everything the pope says, although they may be less enthusiastic when he teaches about social and economic justice. They do not believe that *new* automatically equals *better*.

The church's official prohibition against birth control often serves as a kind of "litmus test" for these Catholics. If you agree with *Humanae Vitae,* the 1968 encyclical of Pope Paul VI forbidding the use of artificial contraceptives, then you are a *true* Catholic. Sometimes they are not happy with the liturgical changes since Vatican Council II, in the mid-1960s. They may or may not belong to or sympathize with Catholic groups that call for a return to the pre-Vatican II Latin Mass, groups whose leaders sometimes encourage members to write to the Vatican complaining about certain "liberal" bishops. Catholics in this category may be called "conservative Catholics."

The final kind of Catholic is the person who tells others that he or she was "raised Catholic" or has "a Catholic background." These people think of themselves as Catholics, but they rarely, if ever, participate in the Eucharist or other sacraments, and they do not belong to a parish community.

Some celebrities—authors, actors, entertainers—and some educators are prominent members of this group. They may have been married in the church, and they may have their children baptized as Catholics, but Catholicism is strictly a peripheral influence on their lives. I call such folks "cultural Catholics."

It's risky to describe the different kinds of Catholics and put labels on them, because the minute you do an exception will come along. A conservative Catholic may be open-minded about liturgical changes, or a liberal Catholic may have a fairly traditional Catholic devotion to the Blessed Mother and/or saints such as St. Anthony or St. Thérèse of Lisieux. Some conservative Catholics are more liberal than others, some liberal Catholics are more conservative than others, and some Sunday Catholics attend Mass every day during Lent. So take my descriptions with a grain of salt, since no particular Catholic is likely to fit any one of my descriptions perfectly. Still, using broad strokes of the brush my overview of the various kinds of Catholics is more accurate than not.

When we address the issue of staying Catholic, each group outlined above would respond differently. A conservative Catholic would say that you can't stay Catholic unless you obey the church's official prohibition of artificial contraceptives and never disagree with anything the pope says. A liberal Catholic might say that in order to stay Catholic all you need do is call yourself a Catholic. Being baptized would be a good idea, but the rest is up to you.

"Whatever grabs ya."

Inevitably, then, I must tip my cards. When I talk about staying Catholic, I refer to a moderate kind of Catholicism. I think of myself as a progressive Catholic with a few liberal, as well as a few conservative leanings, depending on the particular issue. That's the best I can do to describe the kind of Catholic I am. So that I will not be misunderstood, I will go into more detail about what I think it means to be a Catholic.

At rock bottom, I believe that a Catholic is one who can recite the Apostles' Creed and the Nicene Creed as accurate statements of what he or she believes. Together, I would call these two ancient creeds the bottom line. So that we have these "bottom line" statements of faith right in front of us, here they are in a contemporary translation:

The Apostles' Creed

I believe in God, the Father Almighty, creator of heaven and earth. I believe in Jesus Christ, his only Son, our Lord. He was conceived by the power of the Holy Spirit and born of the Virgin Mary. He suffered under Pontius Pilate, was crucified, died, and was buried. He descended to the dead. On the the third day he rose again. He ascended into heaven and is seated at the right hand of the Father. He will come again to judge the living and the dead. I believe in the Holy Spirit, the holy catholic Church, the communion of saints, the forgiveness of sins, the resurrection of the body, and life everlasting. Amen.

The Nicene Creed

We believe in one God, the Father, the Almighty, maker of heaven and earth, of all that is seen and unseen. We believe in one Lord, Jesus Christ, the only Son of God, eternally begotten of the Father, God from God, Light from Light, true God from true God, begotten, not made, one in Being with the Father. Through him all things were made. For us and for our salvation he came down from heaven: by the power of the Holy Spirit he was born of the virgin Mary, and became man. For our sake he was crucified under Pontius Pilate; he suffered, died, and was buried. On the third day he rose again in fulfillment of the Scriptures; he ascended into heaven and is seated at the right hand of the Father. He will come again in glory to judge the living and the dead, and his kingdom will have no end. We believe in the Holy Spirit, the Lord, the giver of life, who proceeds from the Father and the Son. With the Father and the Son he is worshiped and glorified. He has spoken through the Prophets. We believe in one holy catholic and apostolic Church. We acknowledge one baptism for the forgiveness of sins. We look for the resurrection of the dead, and the life of the world to come. Amen.

Of course, members of mainline Protestant churches, such as Lutherans, also recite the Apostles' and Nicene Creeds, so there is nothing particularly Catholic about agreeing with what these creeds contain. To the surprise of many, I suppose, the most basic mark of Catholic identity is not belief in the pope or papal infallibility. As Father Andrew Greeley explains in *The Bottom Line Catechism*, the question that determines Catholic identity is: "Do you believe in God who is revealed to you, however imperfectly, in the Catholic Church that you know? Can you hear his gospel, receive his sacrament, respond to his challenge together with those you love in that church?"

If you answer "Yes" to this line of questioning, then you are a Catholic—of one kind or another. The church's official code of canon law is even more stark. It says that if you were validly baptized and have never formally abandoned Catholicism ("apostatized"), then you are a Catholic.

But, many people would ask, doesn't being a Catholic mean you must obey the official Catholic rules and regulations? When the pope or the bishops say "Jump," don't Catholics have to ask, "How high?" The point is that no one is in a position to judge anyone else's religious obedience. No one can see into anyone else's conscience, into the privacy of his or her life, personal history, and relationship with God.

Still, as Father Greeley comments, if Jesus said, "Let the one who is without sin cast the first stone," some Catholics are more than ready to start throwing. You must obey the church's official teachings, they insist, and if you don't you're a bad Catholic or no Catholic at all—in spite of canon law to the contrary.

But Jesus came to save the imperfect, not the perfect, and he threw up his hands in despair over the legalistic, religious-rules-and-regulations-are-everything Pharisees. Judge not and you will not be judged. That's the perspective of Jesus, although it is not the perspective of some Catholics, and unfortunately sometimes it's not even the perspective of the church's official teachers and guides. So it goes...

A Catholic is one who loves and respects the church all the same. A Catholic is one who can say, in all honesty, "I'm not perfect and neither is the church." A Catholic is one who is baptized, wants to belong to the Catholic Church, finds God in the Catholic community of faith, and finds there forgiveness, spiritual nourishment, courage, healing, and light to live by.

A Catholic is likely to find much wisdom and goodness in many, perhaps most, of the church's laws, but a good Catholic may also find some church rules that, before God, he or she simply cannot accept. To do so would be to violate his or her own conscience. St. Augustine, in the 5th century, said that even if an angel of God should order you to disobey your conscience you should not do so. This does not make you a bad Catholic, and anyone who says it does is a Pharisee in the classic mold.

I recall a wry remark of G. K Chesterton, a convert to Catholicism and probably the most quotable English-speaking Catholic of the 20th century: "Catholics know the two or three transcendental truths on which they do agree; and take rather a pleasure in disagreeing on everything else."

And how.

In the following pages, I will share with you, dear reader, my vision of how to stay Catholic in what I judge to be healthy, holy, delightful ways. I take it for granted that the Catholic faith should bring into one's life peace, joy, and courage, not worry, anxiety, and a grim outlook on life. I have my blind spots, too, so please take my words as a starting point for your own reflections on how to stay Catholic in today's world. Along the way, let us pray for each other, you and I.

Chapter 2

Staying Catholic Yourself

THERE IS much emphasis in the Catholic Church today on what the New Testament calls "koinonia" or "community." People in parish ministries try to "build community" in their parish. Spirituality, we hear, is relational not individualistic. You don't need to attend many church-related workshops or lectures before a speaker frowns with disapproval about the "privatized" piety that held sway before Vatican II, the shake-'em-up church council of the mid-1960s.

All this is true. If anything is clear from the Gospels it is Jesus' conviction that love of God and neighbor cannot be separated. "Those who say, 'I love God,' and hate their brothers or sisters, are liars," says the First Letter of John; "for those who do not love a brother or sister whom they have seen, cannot love God whom they have not seen" (4:20).

Nevertheless, each person is ultimately alone. Each of us is stuck inside his or her own skin. When we die, we die alone. Deep in the core of each person's being he or she is alone with God. It is foolish to deny this, but much about the prevailing culture constitutes just such a denial.

The prevailing culture encourages everyone to follow the crowd. Don't think for yourself, we hear. There is something wrong if you enjoy solitude. Do what "everyone else" does. In our culture, even antisocial forms of behavior—such as a highly peculiar manner of dress or hair style—are alternate ways to conform with one crowd or another.

Each of us must decide what to do with our individuality and our inalienable solitude before God. We are in relation to many other people, and those relationships have a profound impact on our identity. But who we are as individuals has a profound impact on who we are, as well. There is an interdependent connection between individuality and relationality. So, it's important to nourish our individuality—basic to which is one's personal Catholic spirituality—in healthy ways. This chapter will focus on how to stay Catholic on a personal, individual level.

Theologian Father David Tracy, a professor in the Divinity School of the University of Chicago, sheds much light on what's unique and special about being a Catholic. Catholicism has what Tracy calls an "analogical imagination." This means that the stories and images that nourish Catholicism, that Catholics grow up with, take for granted a God who is present in the world. Catholics presume they can find God in and through creation. Indeed, the world, human cultures, and people tend to be rather like God, they are an analogy for God.

The Protestant imagination, Father Tracy continues, is "dialectical." This means that Protestants tend to think of God as absent from the world, or they find God in the world only on rare occasions, particularly in "Jesus Christ, and him crucified" (1 Cor 2:2). For Protestants, the world, human cultures, and people tend to be deeply different from God. God is distant from us and all that we are about.

A Catholic tends to see human societies and cultures as places where God may be found, or where God may find us. A Protestant tends to see these same realities as abandoned by God and therefore of little use or even riddled with sin. For Catholicism, creation and all things human are basically good. For Protestantism, creation and all things human are basically corrupt.

Obviously, there is plenty to support both kinds of imagination. Look how much good there is in the world, and look how much evil there is. Catholicism admits the evil but says that ultimately it's all good, and God is there. Protestantism admits the good but says that ultimately it's all worthless, and God is elsewhere. Of course, you will find Protestants with Catholic leanings and Catholics with Protestant leanings, but these are accurate descriptions of the traditional Catholic and Protestant ways of looking at the world.

To stay Catholic on a personal level calls for efforts to cultivate a vision of life and the cosmos that sees God in as many places, persons, and circumstances as possible.

The most basic place to begin is with oneself, growing in your ability to see God in yourself and in your life. In order to do this, it's important to make time for regular experiences of solitude and silence.

Because our culture encourages us to escape into the crowd and into "group-think," this may seem like an odd suggestion. You will get little support from the spirit of being "with it" if you decide to make regular times for silence and solitude. Yet a deeply Catholic life is almost impossible without such times.

The purpose of silence and solitude is to re-connect with oneself, where God is. You are a "sacrament" of God called through baptism to bring God's love into the world and into other people's lives. Therefore, it is immensely helpful to make times to be alone with the God who lives in you. This is why the traditional Catholic practice of making a silent retreat still has so much going for it. Retreats that involve plenty of personal interaction with other people have their place, but nothing can substitute for a silent retreat.

It can be difficult to find time for a silent retreat, but more often than not it's possible. Few people cannot set aside one weekend a year, for example, to make a silent retreat. Usually, the main obstacle is anxiety. A silent retreat can be an unsettling prospect if, like most Americans, we are addicted to television-watching, random noises, talking, driving a car, being on the move, work, and not sitting still.

Once while I was in the middle of my annual silent retreat at a Trappist monastery, I heard someone's voice outside the window of my room. Glancing out, I saw a classic example of someone who had come to make a retreat but couldn't turn loose of his busy, workaday life. There stood a man talking on a cellular telephone, still doing business in the midst of what was supposed to be a silent retreat.

A silent retreat may last for fifteen minutes, a weekend, a week, or a month. Anyone can find fifteen minutes of quiet in each day for prayerful reflection, and almost anyone can find a way to have a silent retreat at least once a year, even if for only a day or two. What matters is making time to be quiet, sit still, and face the emptiness in yourself where God dwells. Sometimes we can feel God's presence, but often we cannot. Here's the secret: Even when all we can sense is a void, God is there, loving us, healing us, renewing our life, guiding us along the right path. All we need do is be quiet, be still, be open, and abandon ourself to God's love. It's as simple, and sometimes as difficult, as that.

Staying Catholic on a personal level happens in other ways, as well. One of the most basic relates to our vocational decisions. From youth to old age, we face vocational choices. As young adults we typically decide to marry or remain single, and we may ponder the priesthood or life in a religious order or congregation. We try to find work or a career that suits our talents and interests, and this work or career may change several times in a lifetime.

If we are to stay Catholic as we make these choices it's

important to maintain a high awareness of the sacred nature of what we are about. For Catholicism, vocations, careers, and work are not arbitrary or incidental choices. A job or career is not just a way to generate income. Rather, it is a basic way we encounter God in the world and bring the spirit of the gospel into human society. Even if you must accept work that is not satisfying, to pay the rent and put food on the table, it can be a way to express your humanity and spirituality in everyday life, for God is present even in the most boring or difficult job.

As we try to discern the vocation that is best for us, it's important to keep uppermost in mind that we choose not just a way to be in the world but a way to be with God in the world. If we meet someone, fall in love, and decide to marry, that is a choice to make our relationship with God inseparable from our relationship with our spouse. A married Catholic is called to discover God's love in his or her spouse's love. A married Catholic is also called to show God's love to the spouse by loving him or her. In marriage, God loves husband and wife through their love for each other. For Catholics, to identify marriage as one's vocation in life is to choose marriage as the primary way to love God and neighbor. This is what Catholics mean when they say that marriage is a sacrament, not just a contract, personal agreement, or promise. Marriage is a sacrament, a way to be intimate with God by loving one's spouse.

A Catholic who, by choice or happenstance, remains single, can stay Catholic by making that choice a choice to live in ways that focus on God and neighbor. A single person's work can be a way to serve others without as much concern about income as a married person with children. A single person who has a lucrative career or job can stay Catholic by choosing a simpler lifestyle and donating more money to good causes, instead of giving in to cultural pressures to become as affluent and comfortable as possible. A single person can stay Catholic by giving more time to serving those with special needs as a volunteer.

If a Catholic discerns a vocation to the priesthood or religious life, this, too, is a choice to be with God and neighbor in particular ways. These vocations include a choice to be celibate, but this does not mean the person chooses to distance himself or herself from others. Rather, celibacy, like marriage, is a way to be in relation to others. Instead of choosing one special person to relate to, the religioius celibate chooses to be with others on a wider communal basis. A religious celibate chooses to be available to God's people, and he or she chooses to make more time to love God and neighbor in prayer. Indeed, without a major commitment to prayer, the life of a religious celibate takes on less and less meaning as time goes by.

One who would stay Catholic in a career, trade, or other work will choose not just on the basis of salary or the status that may come with a particular kind of work. One who would stay Catholic will choose work with at least the potential to be of service to others. It's possible to choose work that, in itself, is "service-oriented"—a medical pro fession, for example—and still be in it primarily for the high level of affluence it affords. There is nothing Catholic about such an attitude. It's also possible to choose work that has a reputation, deserved or not, for attracting greedy, self-centered people—a business or legal profession, for example—and make it primarily a way to serve others. It's all in your attitude. It's all in whether you make your work a way to love God and neighbor or a way to feather your own nest.

One of the most personal ways to stay Catholic is to look at your calendar and checkbook. How do you spend your time, and how do you spend your money? These are personal matters. Because Catholicism can see God in the most mundane concerns, staying Catholic requires the effort to find God in your hours and days. Sometimes the prevailing culture leads us to spend less time with family and friends, as we could and should. Instead, we work, work, work. We may insist that we do this for our family, but that argument has a hollow ring to it.

Our work is important, to be sure. We serve God and neighbor through our work. Sometimes we must sacrifice family time and time with friends in order to work more. But there comes a point where too much is too much. In our culture, the inclination is always to spend too much time working and not enough time with family and friends. Staying Catholic demands constant vigilance and dedication to keeping a healthy balance between work time and time with those we love.

Staying Catholic as an individual means you try to keep your head screwed on straight from a Catholic perspective. It means making the effort to be a prayerful person and be sensitive to the presence of God in all circumstances. Staying Catholic on a personal level means cultivating the awareness that to be in the world is to be with God, so God is present in all the choices you make and all the experiences you have. Staying Catholic as an individual means you believe with all your heart what St. Augustine said, that God is closer to you than you are to yourself.

Chapter 3

Staying Catholic in Your Relationships

HAVE YOU SEEN either the film or a live stage production of the musical, *Fiddler on the Roof?* Remember the Sabbath scene? Tevye, Golda, and their five daughters—plus the young man who happened by earlier that day—gather around the family table to celebrate the Sabbath. Notice, the family does not climb into Tevye's milk cart for a ride to the synagogue in Anatevka. They stay at home because home is where the most important Sabbath ritual happens, around the family table.

For Catholics, this scene from *Fiddler on the Roof* illustrates the church's spiritual origins. For Catholics—to recall words of Pope John Paul II—the Jews are our elder brothers and sisters. Jesus was a good Jew, and Catholicism's roots are in Judaism. In particular, when Golda, Tevya, and their family gather around the family table to observe the beginning of the Sabbath, this is a sign of how things are supposed to be for Catholics, too.

For centuries before Vatican II, Catholicism almost lost

sight of the fact that the family in its various forms is the most basic unit of the church. Yet this insight goes back as far as the Judeo-Christian tradition goes back. The Hebrew Scriptures are filled with stories about families, from the creation narratives in Genesis to the prophet Hosea. The story of Adam and Eve and their sons Cain and Abel is a family story. The story of Abram and Sarai (later to become Abraham and Sarah) is a story about a family. The story of Noah and the flood is a family story, and so is the story of Moses. Read all these stories again and see. Hosea is a story about faithfulness in marriage that serves as a metaphor for God's faithfulness to his unfaithful people.

The Christian Scriptures, too, include stories about families. The infancy narratives in the Gospels of Matthew and Luke are stories about a very special family's beginnings. Jesus tells stories about family relationships, from the story of the Prodigal Son to the story about Lazarus and his sisters, Mary and Martha. Jesus identifies the characters in his stories by describing them in terms of their family relationships—a widow, a father, a mother, a little daughter, a son. Jesus drew on his own experience of family life to help us understand what our God is like. He said that God is his, and our, loving Papa (*Abba*).

When the Acts of the Apostles and Paul's letters describe where the first Christians gathered to celebrate the Eucharist, they do not tell us that they built themselves a parish church. No, they got together in one another's homes. They were Jewish, after all, so the natural place to gravitate was the home. Jesus borrowed many images from family life, and he said that where two or three, not two hundred or three hundred, gather in his name he would be in their midst. So it was natural for the first Christians to congregate in one another's homes for the Lord's Supper.

Time passed, and even after Christian communities built churches, early theologians wrote about the basic place of family life in the church. In the late 4th century, St. John Chrysostom said that the family is *ekklesia*, using the technical Greek scriptural term for church to describe the family. Christians apparently took this for granted for centuries, until after the Protestant Reformation in the mid-1500s. With the Counter-Reformation launched by the Council of Trent (1545-1563), Catholicism seems to have lost sight of many of its domestic ideals, and Catholicism became parish-centered.

With the rediscovery, at Vatican II, of the ancient tradition that the family is the domestic church, Catholicism began a return to its domestic roots. Today, parish ministers struggle with the practical implications of the truth that family life is the most basic form of church community. If the parish nourishes the church's roots in family life then the parish itself will flourish. In the words of Pope John Paul II, the family is meant to "constitute the church in its fundamental dimension." Families "form the very substance of parish life."

The crucial insight here is that God dwells in human intimacy. When Jesus said that we are to love God with our whole self, and our neighbor as ourself, that was another way to say that love of God and neighbor cannot be separated. We find God first in our neighbor, meaning those we rub elbows with daily—our family, our co-workers, our friends. To stay Catholic requires that we take this insight to heart and act on it.

When Catholicism insists that the family is the most basic unit of the church, this does not mean that single people are left out. On the contrary. The extended family relationships of single adults of any age have a profound impact on their lives. Ask a young single adult what it's like to have married brothers or sisters think of you as a built-in baby sitter. Single adults invariably have a circle of friends that constitute a kind of family for them. The same is true for widowed persons; their extended family is very important to them. In one form or another, family—or, if you prefer, human intimacy—is basic to being a Catholic because close human relationships are basic to human existence.

Clayton C. Barbeau is a well-known Catholic marriage and family therapist, speaker, and author. Barbeau said, "Where you put your time you put your life, and where you put your life you put your love." To stay Catholic we must make time for those closest to us—our spouse, our children, and our friends. We can't say we love these people if we don't share our time with them, for to do this is to love them in spirit and in truth.

The trouble with this line of thought is that it's so contrary to the values the consumer culture pounds into us every day. Ideals of the consumer culture include "rugged individualism," independence, and self-sufficiency. From the consumer culture perspective, you love your family by providing as affluent a lifestyle as possible. Parents show love for their children by buying them almost everything they want. The ideal of the consumer culture is the home as entertainment center, not the home as the center of interpersonal life.

The consumer culture also insists that each family should be independent, needing no one else. The Catholic ideal, on the contrary, insists that God created us for community. As individuals we need friends, and as families we need other families. The Catholic ideal is not independence but interdependence. Staying Catholic depends upon having friends, people we share with on more than a superficial level. The Old High German root for "friend" is *fridu*, peace. A friend is one we can be at peace with, one we don't have to put on an act for.

The primary model for friendship among Christians, of course, is Jesus. In John's Gospel Jesus says: "No one has greater love than this, to lay down one's life for one's friends. You are my friends if you do what I command you. I do not call you servants any longer, because the servant does not know what the master is doing; but I have called you friends, because I have made known to you everything that I have heard from my Father" (5:13-15).

Because we are friends of Jesus, or trying to be, our friendships with one another are grounded in our friendship with Jesus. But, you may say, does it not trivialize our relationship with Jesus to call him our friend? Hardly. St. Richard of Chichester was a 13th-century English saint. He expressed the meaning of friendship with Jesus in words incorporated, more than 700 years later, into the lyrics of a song for the musical, *Godspell:* "O most merciful Friend, my Brother and Redeemer, may I know You more clearly, love You more dearly, and follow You more nearly, day by day, day by day. Amen."

To stay Catholic requires us to spend time with our friends, realizing that in our friends we encounter our Friend, the risen Christ. We need our friends, and our friends need us. If we do not have good friends, we can and should pray, asking our Friend and Brother, Jesus, to help us find good friends. We need friends because, among other things, we need others with whom to share our faith journey. It is difficult to live our Catholic faith authentically, so we need friends to support and encourage us, and we have a need to support and encourage them in return.

For Catholicism, friendship transcends space and time. In both the Apostles' Creed and the Nicene Creed—the two major statements of Christian faith—we profess a belief in "the communion of saints." This means that our *koinonia,* our community, includes believers on earth and in heaven. From the earliest days of the Christian community, believers have had the highest respect and regard for those who died in the faith. This is what it means to "venerate" the saints.

In the first decades of the Christian community, those who died as martyrs for the faith were venerated by the faithful on earth. The early Christians reasoned that if we can pray for one another on earth, it makes perfect sense that those who died heroes of the faith could continue to pray for those they left behind. This is the origin of the Catholic, Orthodox, and—to a lesser extent—Anglican conviction that we may ask saints to help us by their prayers. Since Vatican II, in the mid-1960s, some Catholics have lost touch with the lively tradition of venerating saints. Still, the tradition remains. The Easter Vigil liturgy, for example, includes a litany of petitions to a long list of saints, asking their prayers for the newly baptized. Many Catholics continue to have a strong devotion to saints such as St. Jude, St. Anthony, St. Thérèse of Lisieux, St. Francis of Assisi, and others.

At no time did church doctrine ever insist that the veneration of saints is "necessary for salvation." Quite the opposite. Still, this tradition is one with such ancient origins that to dismiss it entirely would impoverish one's Catholic faith. Dorothy Day was the co-founder of the Catholic Worker movement, and she lived a long life dedicated to peace and the needs of the poor. Dorothy once said that she was "trying to learn to recall my soul like the straying creature that it is as it wanders off over and over again during the day, and lift my heart to the Blessed Mother and the saints, since my occupations are the lowly and humble ones, as were theirs."

This, I think, is one key to the meaning of the veneration of saints. They were ordinary human beings like we are. They struggled to live their faith in the ordinary concerns of everyday life, just as we do. If we believe in the communion of saints, in a community of faith that transcends time and space, then why not be friends with those who enjoy eternal light? Why not ask them to pray for us as we continue our pilgrimage in this world?

A classic Protestant objection insists that to venerate saints detracts from the worship of God and the singular role of Christ as the one mediator between God and people. Clearly, abuses happen. But correctly understood, to venerate saints is spiritually healthy and good for our faith. In the words of the Second Vatican Council's *Dogmatic Constitution on the Church*, ". . .our communion with those in heaven, provided that it is understood in the full light of faith, in no way diminishes the worship of adoration given to God the Father, through Christ, in the Spirit; on the contrary, it greatly enriches it" (art. 51).

I believe that to stay Catholic there needs to be, at the very least, respect for the idea of venerating saints. At best, staying Catholic can be a far richer experience if we include among our circle of friends a few friends in heaven to whom we turn for their prayers. As Vatican II said, to do this can greatly enrich our faith.

The veneration of Mary, the mother of Jesus, has a special

history among Catholics. Technically, she is one of the saints, and sometimes churches and places are named "Saint Mary's." Still, Mary has a special status as the mother of Jesus, so much so that the early church gave her the title, *Theotokos*, Mother of God. Down through the centuries, Mary attracted many forms of devotion, often of ethnic origin. Polish Catholics have a special devotion to the Black Madonna. Hispanic Catholics venerate Our Lady of Guadalupe. European and American Catholics have a traditional devotion to Our Lady of Fatima. The full name of the most prominent Catholic university in the United States is Notre Dame du Lac, French for "Our Lady of the Lake."

Again, to stay Catholic does not require one to have a devotion to the Blessed Mother. Still, I would say that one's Catholic culture may be impoverished without some form of devotion to Mary. For years following Vatican II, I felt no need for such devotion, although Mary had been important to me as I grew up Catholic in the 1950s and '60s. In the early '80s, however, I began to feel a renewed attraction to Mary, especially through the traditional prayer form known as the rosary. Within a couple of years, this rediscovered devotion to the Blessed Mother became the centerpiece of a prayer experience shared with friends.

Once each month, my spouse, Kathy, and I join with several other married couples for prayer and to renew our friendships. We pray the rosary for one another, for our marriages, to nourish our faith, and for the strengthening of marriage and family life in general. We gather with friends to ask our friend, Mary, to pray for us and for the renewal of marriage and family life. For us, this is a genuine experience of the communion of saints. We believers on earth—whom St. Paul called "saints"—come together to be with one another and with all the saints in heaven, with whom we worship God in Christ, our Brother and Friend.

Staying Catholic in our relationships requires effort on several fronts. Essentially, it means making time to be with others. It means making room in our life for family and friends, those here on earth, and those in eternity. Nothing is more Catholic than this.

Chapter 4

Staying Catholic as a Parish

HOW CAN a parish stay Catholic? This may seem like an odd question to ask. Either a parish is Catholic or it's not, is that not so? Certainly a parish is Catholic if it has the right official connections; if it is part of a Catholic diocese; if its chief guide is a Catholic priest or—in the case of a "priest-less parish"—a Catholic permanent deacon or lay pastoral administrator; if the people who make up the parish are Catholics. But to say that this is all that is necessary for a parish to be Catholic is to overlook something crucial. We may ask, Is this parish in touch with living Catholic tradi-tion and the universal church to the extent that it could and should be? Is the parish staff in touch with the lives of the people that make up the parish? Are parish leaders aware of what a Catholic parish must be if it is to thrive in the 21st century?

If the staff and volunteer leaders—members of the parish council, and so forth—were to stand in the sanctuary of their parish church any Sunday morning, facing the congregation, what would they see? Would they see a congregation made up of people related to one another only in incidental ways?

If we shake the scales from our eyes, we will realize that every parish Sunday Mass is populated with people who are not there alone. Most are there with other family members, and frequently whole famlies are there together. This signifies a reality parish staff and volunteer leaders often overlook—namely, that the parish faith community is made up of many smaller faith communities— families, mostly, plus other small-group relational networks. If a parish is to be truly Catholic, it must not take this fact lightly. Many parishes either overlook or take for granted the domestic churches that constitute the parish community, but that is changing. Looking to the dawn of a new century, parishes are beginning to realize that we may no longer take families for granted.

God lives with people. There is no more Catholic insight than this one. It means that we do not find God apart from our most significant human relationships; rather, we find God in various forms of human intimacy. The overwhelming majority of the people who make up a parish encounter God most often in the hurly-burly of family life—in traditional two-parent families, in single-parent families, in marriages without children, in so-called "blended" families, and for single and widowed adults, in their extended families. Therefore, if the parish is to serve its rightful purpose it must place a high priority on the nourishment and support of human relationships.

Time after time, responding to invitations to speak in parishes and to larger groups at national meetings, Catholics tell me that the source of their deepest joy and most painful anguish is their family relationships. There is no greater joy than the joy family life gives us, and there is no more profound suffering than the suffering we get from family life. From a Catholic faith perspective, this means that it is in family life that we have our most intense experiences of cross and resurrection. How can a parish, then, neglect the need to nourish, support, and celebrate family life? How can a parish staff take for granted people's family relationships and think they are fulfilling the mission of the parish to exist solely "for the good of souls" (Vatican II, *Decree on the Bishops' Pastoral Office in the Church*, art. 31)?

Pope John Paul II, while on a visit to the United States, declared that families "form the very substance of parish life." To stay Catholic, a parish must have a family perspective on all that it does, from liturgies to finances; from religious education to hospital visits; from Catholic schools to social outreach ministries. There is no aspect of parish life that does not have a family dimension, and to stay Catholic a parish must be aware of and in touch with this family dimension. Otherwise, the parish is out of touch with its own roots, which are in family life and other forms of human intimacy. But that's not all.

It is the unique role of the parish to preserve Catholic

culture and explore new ways to bring that culture alive for people. Since Vatican II, in response to the need to "get back to the basics" in many areas of church life, countless parishes put the spotlight on the Eucharist as the heart of parish life, and rightly so. But as we slip-slide toward the beginning of a new century it seems time to reincorporate, in a balanced and spiritually healthy fashion, some of the Catholic traditions we tossed into a closet after Vatican II. The idea is not simply to dust off the old paraphernalia and start using it again. The idea is to give new life to traditions that deserve to be rescued from possible oblivion.

Let me put it as bluntly as possible. Catholicism thrives on cultural and spiritual multiplicity. Catholicism thrives on finding God all over the place. James Joyce, himself a "lapsed Catholic," understood this well. When Joyce described the church, he said, "Here comes everybody." That's what Catholicism is about, everybody and everything. Calvinism is stark and severe. Catholicism is wild and crazy. Calvinism strips the church bare. Catholicism fills the church with bright colors, pictures, music, sweet smells, images, and flowers. Calvinism denies the senses. Catholicism fills the senses to overflowing.

Sometimes newer parish church interiors are designed without a prominent crucifix. Instead, you find a bare cross or an image of the risen Christ. The theology implied by this choice is terrible; it's out of touch with the everyday lives of the people who constitute the parish. Catholics put a crucifix in their churches because they understand the basic place of the cross in human experience.

Human suffering finds meaning in the image of the crucified Jesus, which says that suffering is an unavoidable part of life. A crucifix says that the Son of God shares that suffering. People don't have a difficult time understanding or accepting the joy in their lives. With that they need no help. People find it difficult to accept suffering and anguish, and with that they need some help. That is why Catholics are perplexed, sometimes angry, when a new parish church does not have a crucifix prominently displayed.

An image of the risen Christ is theologically legitimate, in itself, but to substitute it for a crucifix is spiritually redundant to the point of crass insensitivity to the lives of ordinary people. In order to stay Catholic, a parish church interior should have a crucifix large enough so people can see it easily.

Let us welcome the recovery of Catholic culture in our parishes when accomplished with intelligence and common sense. Give us back saints, angels, the Blessed Mother, and church interiors that appeal to and awaken or excite our sight, smell, taste, touch, and hearing. Give us back holy water, the crucifix and other sacramentals, holy cards, popular devotions, and sacred gestures, such as genuflecting out of respect for the Blessed Sacrament. Give us back ethnic Catholic traditions. Give us back the chance to worship with our body. For to do all this is to give us back the Incarnation, the mystery of a God "who sent his only Son into the world so that we might live through him" (1 Jn 4:9). Apart from a sensuous Catholic culture the Incarnation remains little more than a "mind trip."

To stay Catholic, parishes should attend to the recovery of traditional devotions. By all means the Eucharist should retain pride of place and be the central gathering of the parish community for prayer and worship. But for heaven's sake, that doesn't mean the parish can't gather for other forms of communal prayer, as well. Why not resurrect and revivify traditional Catholic devotions to Mary, the mother of Jesus, and to various saints?

Parish communal devotions to Mary or popular saints such as St. Jude or St. Anthony touch people and nourish their spirituality in perfectly legitimate ways. Parish staff may worry that such devotions contradict the spirit of Vatican II, but worry not. The authentic cult of the saints consists in "a more intense practice of our love, whereby, for our own greater good and that of the church, we seek from the saints example in their way of life, fellowship in their communion, and the help of their intercession" (Vatican II, *Dogmatic Constitution on the Church*, art. 51).

The council was equally positive about devotion to Mary. While it cautioned against abuses and theologically un-balanced attitudes, the council urged that "the cult, especially the liturgical cult, of the Blessed Virgin, be generously fostered, and that the practices and exercise of devotion towards her. . . be highly esteemed. . ." (*Dogmatic Constitution on the Church*, art. 67).

To stay Catholic, there should be more opportunities in a parish for communal prayer than Mass on Sunday. To stay Catholic, a parish should give people opportunities to enrich their faith by weekday evening communal devotions to the Blessed Mother and various saints. May is the traditional month dedicated to Mary, so communal recitations of the rosary—perhaps a scriptural version—are appropriate. When hard times hit, offer communal devotions to St. Jude, the patron of hopeless situations. Parishes that schedule a novena to St. Anthony often find that many people attend. Update traditional devotional services with heavy in-put from scripture and a brief sermon that helps people to put their devotion to Mary or the saint in a balanced perspective.

"Piety" has gotten a bad rap. The word simply means "religious devotion and reverence to God," but to some it implies excessive religious sentimentality—in brief, spiritual sappiness. To stay Catholic, a parish should be a place that nourishes people's piety, their sense of being dedicated or devoted to Christ, and their understanding of themselves as members of a community of faith. Ah, but what are the most effective ways to do this?

Many parish leaders knock themselves out giving people a chance to gain a better understanding of their faith through adult religious education, lectures, that sort of thing. Typically during Lent, for example, parishes schedule a series of speakers. Typically, only a small minority attend. Speakers are fine, and God knows many Catholics need all the intellectual up-dating they can get. Still, Lent is a time for more than cognitive jumping jacks and push-ups. Lent is about what the New Testament calls *metanoia,* a radical personal transformation, conversion, repentance. What is more likely to nourish a rededication to one's faith, a lecture or a chance to nourish one's piety? Does one demand the elimination of the other?

After Vatican II, Catholic parishes virtually abandoned a traditional Eucharistic devotion called "Benediction of the Blessed Sacrament." I humbly suggest that to stay Catholic parishes need to rethink this devotion. If Catholicism is anything, it's Eucharistic. The Eucharist is the center of Catholic life, the "summit and source" of Catholic life. With Vatican II, the emphasis is on the Eucharist as "action," as a communal ritual, something we do together. The Mass is not a private devotional activity. We stress the connection between the Eucharist and the faith we live in the everyday world. We insist today that the Eucharistic bread is not mainly to worship but to eat.

Granted, and whole-heartedly. Nevertheless, to stay Catholic parishes should revive some form of that traditional devotion, Benediction of the Blessed Sacrament. The Catholic spirit needs not only the liturgy of the Eucharist, but a chance to cultivate a Eucharistic piety, a sense of reverence for Christ present in the consecrated bread and wine we consume at Mass. Benediction of the Blessed Sacrament can be a time to reflect upon what we do at the Eucharistic liturgy and nourish our appreciation and understanding.

Benediction can include a short sermon that helps people to understand the Eucharist better. It can nourish people's respect for the holiness of what we do at Mass. Perhaps Benediction of the Blessed Sacrament can help us to regain, in a healthy way, some of the experience of transcendence during the Eucharist that is largely absent nowadays.

Lest you should, gentle reader, get the impression that I encourage a retrograde parish movement ("Turn back the clock!") that would abandon the many positive developments in parish life since Vatican II, please be reassured. The task before parishes today is to gird up their collective loins for the future. To survive in that future, parishes will need, first, to have a family perspective and be dedicated to the support of family and small community life. Second, parishes will need to be places where Catholic culture is alive and ready to nourish a rich, healthy Catholic spirituality and piety.

To stay Catholic, the goal is not for a parish to return to the past. The goal is for the parish to gather up its resources, including Catholicism's cultural traditions, and face the future with courage and imagination.

Chapter 5

Staying Catholic in the Workplace

SOMETIMES it sets people back a notch or two when they hear that there is a spirituality of work. For many generations Catholics thought of spirituality as a term with little meaning in the everyday world, particularly in the workplace.

Once a year, Catholics might hear a sermon on St. Joseph, patron of workers, and the dignity of work, but that was about it. Work was a secular or "profane" concern. Indeed, was not work part of God's punishment for original sin? "Sweat of your brow," and all that?

Not exactly. "God blessed them," says Genesis 1:28, "and God said to them, '. . . fill the earth and subdue it . . .' " In other words, work was part of God's creation before Adam's and Eve's prideful disobedience. God meant work to be a blessing.

"And on the seventh day God finished the work that he had done," says Genesis 2:2, "and he rested on the seventh day from all the work that he had done." Genesis describes the divine act of creation as "work." Therefore, to work is to follow the example of the Creator, which means that work is holy.

Later in the story, we find these words: "And to the man [God] said, "Because you have listened to the voice of your wife, and have eaten of the tree about which I commanded you, 'You shall not eat of it,' cursed is the ground because of you; in toil you shall eat of it all the days of your life. . . By the sweat of your face you shall eat bread. . ." (Gen 3:17, 19). After the Fall, survival depends upon hard work, whereas before the Fall work was a kind of holy play.

There are three perspectives to keep in mind. First, in the beginning work was part of God's blessing on human beings; indeed, work is holy because to work is to imitate the Creator.

Second, after the Fall, God's punishment means that survival will depend upon strenuous work. Still, there is nothing in the creation narratives to suggest that work is no longer holy and a blessing, too.

Third, after the Incarnation, the coming of the Son of God into the world, all things are new, including work. "So if anyone is in Christ," Paul says, "there is a new creation: everything old has passed away; see, everything has become new" (2 Cor 5:17)!

Following the sin of Adam and Eve a dark shadow fell across human work, but Christian faith enables us to begin disengaging from this dark shadow. Now, the light of Christ begins to illumine work so it can become, once again, the blessing it was meant to be.

From a Christian perspective, work is a way to live one's faith, a way to act on one's spirituality, and a way to prepare for the final coming of God's kingdom. Work, as much as anything else, is a way to love God and neighbor. Each person's work is part of the way God calls him or her to bring into the world the spirit of the good news about God's love and forgiveness. Through the blessing of work we can make the world a better place. Staying Catholic requires that we do all we can to do our work with a faith-filled heart. Not only that, but from a Catholic perspective we can find God in our work. To stay Catholic requires us to be about our work with faith and on the alert for the presence of God's love.

For Catholicism, work is not just a way to "make a living," although it is that, too, of course. Work is also meant to be a source of God's self-gift or grace. In our work, no matter what it may be, we can grow closer to God if we are aware of the spirituality of our work. Nothing is more Catholic than this.

This, basically, is the Catholic perspective on work. Still, powerful cultural and social influences shape our feelings and thoughts about work, as well. The kinds of work that are available have tremendous impact on how we think about work, as do economic systems and the policies of employers. Work is a complex part of human existence. The key to staying Catholic is to keep uppermost in mind that God means work to be a blessing, even though sometimes work is difficult and even dehumanizing. Even the most arduous, seemingly senseless work can have meaning if we do it with love. A man who works two jobs cleaning office buildings, for example, may do that work with love because he does it so his children may attend a Catholic high school or get a college education.

There are so many different kinds of work that it is impossible to deal with all of them. We hear about white collar work, blue collar work, professions, jobs, and careers, but whatever these distinctions may imply they all constitute work, and each kind of work has a unique spirituality. There is a spirituality appropriate to a minimum-wage job in a fast-food restaurant, and there is a spirituality appropriate for insurance agents, janitors, and automobile mechanics. A cab driver has a spirituality, and so do a brain surgeon and a construction worker. An attorney who is in touch with the Christian spirituality of his or her work will go about being an attorney in a special fashion. A farmer in touch with the spirituality of farming will find meaning in his or her work that someone not in touch with that spirituality will miss.

Some kinds of work seem natural ways to serve others, to love God and neighbor. Teachers seem to have this kind of work. Still, it is just as possible for a teacher to be self-centered and greedy as it is for anyone else. A teacher can merely put in his or her time, doing what's required but nothing more, with little concern for students as unique individuals. A teacher can seek a position based on income considerations alone.

Other kinds of work have a reputation for attracting greedy, profit-obsessed people. Lawyers fit this category, yet there is just as much potential to serve God and neighbor as a lawyer as there is in any other line of work.

The same is true for people in business. What products and/or services does a particular business person provide for the rest of us? What are the business person's attitudes toward the people who buy his or her products or services? The business person's spirituality shows itself in ways such as these.

Businesses provide employment for many people. How do business owners and managers relate to their employees? If economic pressures require a corporate manager to let an employee go, how does he or she do this? In a sensitive and caring manner with the emloyee's needs in mind, or with an impersonal note and no personal contact? This speaks volumes about the corporate manager's spirituality.

There is also a Catholic spirituality for unemployment. At one time or another almost everyone must cope with being out of work. How does one go about maximizing one's Catholic faith at such a time? The basic assumption is this: If God is present in all situations, then it is possible to find God in a special way in the experience of being unemployed. God is there, it's up to us to be open to the unique way in which the Divine Mystery is manifest in this situation.

Bill, a man in his mid-thirties, worked for an advertising firm for fifteen years. He did his work well and received promotions within the firm. The head of the division Bill supervised called him into his office one day, out of the blue, and informed him that the word had come down that his division was being phased out for economic reasons. Bill and the five people he was responsible for were being let go. Bill's supervisor was sorry, but his hands were tied. Bill would receive six months' severance pay, which was generous under the circumstances. That was it.

Bill was devastated. What had happened to his life? What would he do? Where would he go? His wife's job seemed secure, but her salary alone could not pay the family's expenses. "I felt like a cold wind had come into my life," Bill recalled, "and the world had become a dark and forbidding place."

The first week, after Bill's wife and children were gone for the day, he could do little more than sit and stare into space, or stumble aimlessly around the house. Bill's mood shifted from anger to resignation and back again several times each day. After two weeks, Bill's wife suggested he talk with Tony, a friend who had been unemployed a couple of years earlier. Tony suggested that Bill try what had been the greatest help to him while he looked for work.

"I don't know what you'll think of this," Tony said, "but after about a month of knocking my head against the wall I came across my old rosary in the back of my socks drawer. I took it out and began to pray the rosary a couple of times each day while I was alone. It gave me something to do that seemed to have more value than just sitting around feeling sorry for myself. In the end, the rosary gave me the energy to get off my duff and do something about my problem. I started attending daily Mass, too, and that made a big difference in my attitude."

Unemployment is no fun. But to stay Catholic, and tap into one's Catholic faith while unemployed, we need to be on the lookout for God even in unemployment. That's what Bill did. He took Tony's advice, and before long he was in the public library researching new job directions, services available, and other options. Soon Bill felt better and had a more hopeful outlook. He discovered a government program that would enable him to retrain for another job, and along the way he found that he could market his advertising skills on a freelance basis to bring in some badly needed income. Five months after he lost his job, Bill found a new position, which he attributes to prayer and his own diligence.

"You may find this hard to believe," Bill said, "but being unemployed was a good thing for me. It brought me closer to God, and closer to my wife and children. In a way, it was a real blessing."

Work is an important part of life. To stay Catholic in the midst of work—or its absence—requires a heart attuned to God's presence in the ordinary circumstances of everday life. There is nothing more Catholic than the ability to do this with persistence and a loving heart.

"Catholic is Wonderful!"

MILLING ABOUT in the after-Mass crowd one Sunday morning, I paused to chat with a friend who teaches theology at a Catholic university. As we brought each other up-to-date on what had been happening in our lives during the previous week, I mentioned that I was working on a book on staying Catholic. "That's a good idea for a book," my friend said. "Over the last few years I discovered a renewed sense of how much I enjoy being a Catholic. Catholic is wonderful! We should appreciate our Catholic identity and heritage more than we sometimes do. It's fine to appreciate other Christian traditions, but we should value what's special about being Catholic, too."

Many times since this chance conversation, I have recalled my friend's words: "Catholic is wonderful!" Catholicism has its shadow side, of course. It's isn't perfect, and it would be arrogant and dishonest to claim otherwise. But so much about Catholicism is so good. As churches go, it has far more going for it than against it. It is, after all, not just an ordinary institution but one rooted in salvation history with ideals and goals found no place else. The church isn't divine, but its focus is.

We should stop and think about this more often. Catholicism has a culture all its own, some of which many Catholics neglected in the decades following Vatican II. Catholicism has a rich intellectual heritage that many young Catholics don't know much about. Catholicism has a tradition of respect for the arts, too. Some of the greatest contributions to western civilization came from Catholicism's appreciation of music, architecture, and literature.

People who trek off into eastern spiritualities—Buddhism, Zen, Hinduism—in search of an inner path, don't often realize that the mystical tradition in Catholicism has even more to offer. The spiritual tradition represented by St. John of the Cross and St. Teresa of Avila in the sixteenth century, and Thomas Merton in the twentieth, runs deep and clear.

In *St. Thomas Aquinas: The Dumb Ox*, G. K. Chesterton used a tree as a metaphor. He wrote that for Aquinas "the point is always that Man is not a balloon going up into the sky, nor a mole burrowing merely in the earth; but rather a thing like a tree, whose roots are fed from the earth, while its highest branches rise almost to the stars."

The same is true of Catholicism, which is like a great old oak tree, "whose roots are fed from the earth, while its highest branches reach almost to the stars." That's what it means to be a Catholic, and it truly is wonderful.

Suggestions for Further Reading

Catholicism, by Richard P. McBrien. Revised Edition, 1994. HarperSanFrancisco. The best reference work available in English.

Time Capsules of the Church, by Mitch Finley. Our Sunday Visitor Books, 1990. There is nothing like historical insights to put the present in a balanced perspective. A brief, informative look at ten moments in church history that still have an impact on Catholic life today.

What Are the Theologians Saying NOW? by Monika K. Hellwig. Christian Classics, 1992. A great popular overview of contemporary Catholic theology.

The Catholic Myth: The Behavior and Beliefs of American Catholics, by Andrew M. Greeley. Scribners, 1990. A fascinating, informative look at what today's Catholics really believe.

Why Be Catholic? by Richard Rohr, O.F.M. and Joseph Martos. St. Anthony Messenger Press, 1989. A delightful response to the question the book's title asks.

We hope you enjoyed this book. To receive a Resurrection Press catalog call 800-89 BOOKS.